D0831979

THE SIMPLE GUIDE TO
TURKEY
CUSTOMS AND ETIQUETTE

ABOUT THE AUTHOR

DAVID SHANKLAND is Lecturer in Social Anthropology at the
University of Wales, Lampeter. He was previously Assistant and
Acting Director at the British Institute of Archaeology in Ankara,
and has been visiting lecturer at the Middle East Technical
University, Ankara. He has travelled, worked and researched
extensively in Turkey. As well as many scholarly papers, he is the
author of *Islam and Society in Turkey*, and is currently conducting
research at Çatalhöyük, in the Konya plain.

ILLUSTRATED BY
IRENE SANDERSON

SIMPLE GUIDE TO

TURKEY

CUSTOMS & ETIQUETTE

DAVID SHANKLAND

GLOBAL BOOKS LTD

Simple Guides • Series 1
CUSTOMS & ETIQUETTE

The Simple Guide to
TURKEY
CUSTOMS & ETIQUETTE
by David Shankland

First published 1992 by Simple Books Ltd

Second Edition 1999 by
GLOBAL BOOKS LTD
PO Box 219, Folkestone, Kent, England CT20 3LZ

ⓒ Global Books Ltd 1999

ISBN 1–86034–001–6

British Library Cataloguing in Publication Data
A CIP catalogue entry for this book
is available from the British Library

Set in Futura 11 on 12 pt by Bookman, Hayes, Middlesex
Printed in Malta by Interprint Ltd

Contents

Map of Turkey

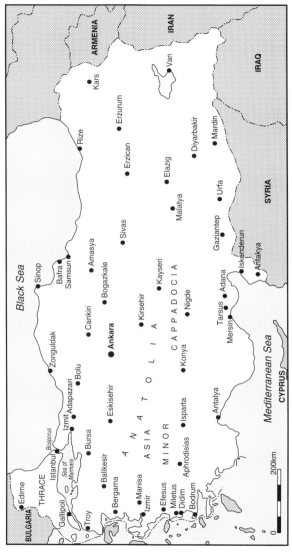

Village life

Foreword

For centuries, Turkey has fascinated Western travellers. On their return, many have written books telling of the marvels of Istanbul (Constantinople), the glories of the Sultan's court and the strength of his army. Turkey retains its power to delight the visitor. But that very power is also a cause of confusion. The language is strange, with few familiar words. Friendships are made and lost through ways not apparent. Business arrangements are agreed then fall through for no obvious reason. In short, whilst in Turkey the visitor cannot but suspect that the rules of etiquette are very different from those he or she is used to.

With care, these differences can be overcome. Certain factors are of great importance when trying to empathize with Turkish life; the Republican heritage, the depth of the Islamic culture, the pattern of social relations, and the long tradition of hospitality. This book has been written to highlight these factors, so that moments when you say 'That is not what I meant at all!' occur as rarely as possible.

FOREWORD TO THE SECOND EDITION

This second edition appears seven years after the first. During this time, Turkey has changed greatly. The Customs Union with Europe has been completed successfully. Though inflation is high, the economy, particularly the private sector, has expanded steadily. Islam has grown as an important political force, and the sad conflict in the east has claimed many lives. However, Turkey remains just as exciting as before, if not more so, and the commitment by the vast majority of the population to democracy and to the fruits of modernization and technology lend it more stability than is sometimes realized.

Traditional culture and etiquette is resilient in many ways. Scrupulous attention to dress, to good manners, to social relations still reaps enormous benefits, and the warmth with which people will return any effort to learn a few words of Turkish makes such an attempt worthwhile many times over.

D.S.

1

The Land

Carved relief on Yakutiye Medrese, Erzurum

On the map, Turkey largely appears as a rectangle situated just off the south-east of Europe, an area formerly known in the West as Asia Minor, but today as 'Anatolia'. Turkey's territory also extends into Europe, giving her a border with Greece and Bulgaria. Istanbul, now a city of perhaps ten million people, straddles both the European and the Asian sides, and is divided by the Bosphorus straits.

Geographically, Anatolia remains the heart-land of Turkey. Flanked by the Black Sea to the north, the Aegean to the west and the Mediterranean to the south, the sea lends a natural coherence to this enormous land mass. To the east, the land border comprises of a shared frontier successively with Georgia, Armenia, Iran, Iraq and Syria. This combination of long coast-line yet diverse neighbours means that Turkey is at once distinctive and closely bound up with the political pre-occupations of the region.

Anatolia has long been the place of enduring and varied civilizations. One of the earliest and most sophisticated Neolithic peoples known was discovered in the nineteen sixties at Çatal-höyük, in the Konya plain. More than eight thousand years ago, these people had developed farming, textiles, and domestic art to a degree that is surprising archaeologists still today.

Hot Tip: Biggest Collection of Classical Remains

Turkey's rich heritage can be traced through the Hittites, Sumerians, the Ancient Greeks and Romans. Indeed, it is the (accurate) claim of the Turkish Tourist Office that there are more classical remains in Turkey than in any other country.

The land became Turkish through a series of tribal invasions from the east dating from the beginning of the second millennium. It was a slow process, the Byzantines gradually, and painfully gave up their territory over several centuries. One notable Islamic civilization, the Seljuks, made their capital in Konya, where remains of their mosques and palaces can still be seen. They gave way to the Ottomans, who formed a base for a hundred years in Bursa. Finally, the Ottomans conquered Constantinople in 1453.

Making this glorious city the centre of their new Empire, the Ottomans proceeded to expand through the Mediterranean and into Europe, at the furthest extent reaching the gates of Vienna, being beaten back finally in 1684. This was the peak of their success. Declining slowly, the Ottomans gradually lost territory until by the time of the First World War, they were often characterized as being the 'Sick Man of Europe'. Under the leadership of the revolutionary movement known as the 'Young Turks', they joined the German side in the First World War. This disastrous decision resulted ultimately in their capitulation, and the occupation of Istanbul by the Allies in 1918.

MODERN TURKEY

Modern Turkey was formed during these uncertain years. Whilst her present-day borders were substantially recognized at the Treaty of Lausanne, signed on 24 July 1923, it was not an easy struggle. The allies, confident in their victory, had decided to share different parts of Anatolia amongst themselves and began to occupy their mandated territory accordingly. A nationalist movement in Ankara, led by Mustafa Kemal (later known as Atatürk), negotiated the departure of the Italian and French in the south, suppressed uprisings by the Kurds and the Armenians in the east, repulsed the Greeks in the west, and threatened the allies occupying Istanbul with conflict in the city itself before Turkey gained acceptance of its right to self-government.

The Republic that emerged is greatly different from the Ottoman Empire. Its capital is Ankara, not Istanbul. Rather than being ruled by a Sultan, sovereignty is vested in a Grand National Assembly, the sole legislative authority. The Caliphate has been abolished. The Arabic script, in which Ottoman was written, has been replaced by the Latin alphabet. The Turkish language has been purged of words of Arabic or Persian derivation, and new words invented to take their place.

These were part of a coherent package of reforms devised by Atatürk to make Turkey a modern country based on those of Western Europe at that time. Part of Atatürk's programme of reforms was devoted to making Turkey secular, that is to say he separated governing the country from religious doctrines. The present-day legal system is based on a combination of the Swiss, German and Italian codes, and a person's private beliefs are distinguished from their business or official transactions.

Hot Tip: Turkey's Western Orientation

In many ways, Atatürk's desires have been fulfilled. Whilst Turkey has pursued a policy of active neutrality with all her neighbours, she has remained oriented firmly towards the West. She is a member of NATO, the Council of Europe, and has been an associate member of the European Union for many years. Recently, the European Union seems to have rebuffed her desire to become a full member, but the Customs Union has gone ahead. Since it has been established, trade with Europe has more than doubled, showing the practical success of this move.

Modern Turkey has also succeeded in becoming a democracy. Much of the apparatus to achieve this transition had been put in place by Atatürk who remained president until his death in 1938. He insisted on the primacy of the Grand National Assembly as the key decision-making body in the country. He did not seek to quell debate; the laws that he conceived were argued vociferously in the Assembly. The Republican Peoples' Party, the party that he had founded to implement his reforms, was frequently fractious, and far more than simply a reflection of his views. Nevertheless, the first general elections in the new Republic took place only after the Second World War, in 1946. The government changed in 1950, when the opposition party swept into power with a massive majority. Since then there have been general elections at regular intervals.

In spite of a presumption that the military would be able to keep aloof from the daily running of the country, this has not come about. There have been *coups* of varying degrees of severity in 1960, 1971 and 1980. Paradoxically, on each occasion, the army has returned democracy to the country, and elections have re-commenced. The army would certainly claim that their interventions have been necessary to reprieve the Republic from internal social conflict and to protect the Kemalist reforms. Should they feel it necessary, they will no doubt intervene again, though it is equally likely that they will again return power to the civilians.

Ankara

ANKARA – THE NEW CAPITAL

Throughout the seventy-five years of the Republic there has been steady industrial development. At the founding of the Republic in 1923, Turkey's economy was rudimentary. Almost 85 per cent of the people lived in villages that relied on technology that had hardly changed for thousands of years. Ankara, Turkey's new capital, was little more that a cluster of worn-out houses beneath a hill on which lay a ruined castle. Today, Turkey's economy is booming. The majority of the population live in urban areas, in conditions that their grandparents would not have dreamt possible. Ankara is now a flourishing city of several million people, and as a firm promise of its determination to get things done, boasts an ultra modern underground train network that is cheap, clean, quiet and efficient.

The one great flaw in this success has been the situation in the east of the country. Over the last two decades a serious battle in the mountainous areas has been taking place between the army forces and the PKK. The PKK are a terrorist Marxist organization which has succeeded in focusing and stimulating Kurdish tribal opposition to the Turkish state. This tragic and brutal conflict has not spread throughout the rest of Turkey, and therefore poses no danger to the business or casual traveller. It should also be noted that whilst the state has acted severely against separatist aspirations, being Kurdish in itself is not subject to discrimination. More than half the Kurdish population now lives in the west of Turkey, particularly in Istanbul and Ankara, and many Kurdish people have senior positions in the bureaucracy and in politics.

2

The People

Atatürk

ATATÜRK'S HERITAGE

Even on the briefest trip to Turkey, the visitor will be struck by the continuing presence of Kemal Atatürk. His picture hangs in shops, work places and government buildings. On national holidays his portrait is suspended high from office blocks. Every town square has his statue. Roads, stadiums, sports halls, schools, even towers and dams are named after him. Lessons on his life are compulsory in schools, reputations are made out of scholarly dissertations on his writings.

It would be quite mistaken to regard this veneration as imposed by the government. The institutions and ideals which Atatürk created remain substantially unchanged to this day. Indeed, now that the Soviet Union is no more, his reforms represent perhaps the most long-lived and successful attempt at social engineering in history. Through them, Turks experience the elements of a modern Western nation: nation ballet and opera companies, national museums and libraries; universities and learned bodies and a parliament.

Today, visitors to Turkey are sometimes surprised to see that women in the cities are usually dressed in the latest fashions, often very *chic*. This is a direct result of Atatürk's desire that women should play a full part in the life of the modern nation that he was founding. Indeed, not just in dress, but also in enabling women to study, to vote, to pursue a professional career Turkey has been at the forefront of female emancipation in Europe. In the early 1990s, Mrs Tansu Çiller became Turkey's first woman Prime Minister. That she did so is no coincidence, but builds on this long acceptance of women in the public life of the country.

TURKEY'S ISLAMIC TRADITIONS

Nevertheless, evidence of the country's Islamic character is all around, and etiquette might be said to begin with respecting its customs. Turks, like other Islamic peoples, pray in a mosque (*cami*).

Hot Tip: Behaviour in a Mosque

Non-Muslims are always welcome in a mosque, but it is polite to wait until a service has ended before entering. Shoes must be taken off and only put on again after leaving the mosque. Whilst inside, women are usually asked to cover their heads with a scarf and both men and women must be decently dressed.

Inside a mosque

Tourists are free to explore the mosque. Photography is usually permitted. Tourists must not, however, approach the covered galleries which line the rear of the interior (these are reserved for Muslim women) nor the *mihrab*, the niche facing Mecca from which the mosque official, the *imam*, leads the prayer. If the *imam* has welcomed you to the mosque, or guided you around it, then he will expect a tip. The equivalent of £2 ($3.50) is sufficient. He does not put this money into his own pocket, but into a fund for the mosque's upkeep.

In recent years, the political party devoted to Islam, *Refah Partisi* (usually known in English as the Welfare Party) has been growing in popularity. In 1994, they took control of the municipalities of Istanbul and Ankara, and after the general elections in December 1995 became the largest political party in the Assembly. In 1996, they provided the prime minister, Necmettin Erbakan, with a coalition government. Then, after several very uneasy months, the constitutional court found their activities to be unlawful, and the party was suspended. It has re-opened under the name 'Virtue Party' (*Fazilet Partisi*), and continues its activities though Erbakan and several of his closest supporters have been debarred from playing an active political role.

Given the popularity of the Islamic movement, it is quite likely that you will come across its supporters during your stay. Men who adhere to this movement are likely to be carefully, even scrupulously dressed. Women who are part of it, whilst they rarely wear a veil, do wear a particular type of headscarf and often also a long coat so that their hair, ankles and wrists are concealed. Paradoxically, whatever their political beliefs, they are not usually difficult people to deal with. Whilst it is possible to doubt their commitment to a pluralistic society (and therein lie their difficulties with the courts), it is clear that they are committed to modern technology, and are invariably enthusiastic and courteous in their everyday dealings with visitors from the West.

Even though the place of religion in politics is one of the most important topics of the day, in general conversation it is not considered polite to inquire as to a person's religious belief. Unless the subject is brought up it is safe to assume that one's acquaintance is not fanatical but respectful of the country's religious traditions. Even if religion does arise, it is perhaps wise to avoid theological debates, which can become very detailed and long-winded.

Hot Tip: Be Tactful!

Turkish people are very fond of welcoming people from other countries, and are often fascinated by the news that they have to tell. Nevertheless, they are equally sensitive to the image that they purvey and detest being thought of as backward, or as in any way inferior. Thus, whilst they themselves might criticize, say, their town planning compared with that of Germany's, it is not tactful for a visitor to say so until he/she has formed a very close friendship.

A lso bear in mind the widespread admiration for Atatürk. His secular reforms have now become controversial, but as a nation-builder his fame and reputation are assured. One of the most frequent of all slogans, *Ne mütlü Türküm diyene*, 'How happy is he or she who can say, I am Turkish!' is much more than an empty phrase, it genuinely reflects most Turkish peoples' inner belief and their commitment to Turkey as a nation. For this reason, it is deeply impolite even foolhardy to criticize Atatürk or to disparage his image. In the late eighties, a public row ensued when an American sailor after a night out in a small port in the south, relieved himself over a statue of the great man. The locals were only prevented from lynching the sailor by the police, who were loudly abused for their lack of patriotism.

I f Islam and the labels of modern nationhood are respected, the visitor can be assured of making new friends, and of delightfully varied experiences; moving from mosque to art gallery, bazaar to shop, concert hall to traditional wedding, he will be continually struck by the dynamic, varied and creative synthesis between the Muslim and Western worlds.

3

Social Relations

Rural home

Turkish people tend to feel personally responsible for the success of a visitor's stay. Just after I arrived for the first time, I inadvertently plugged the telephone into the electricity socket. Not knowing where to go to have the charred item repaired, I got into a taxi and showed it to the driver. He took me to the main telecommunications building, whereupon the doormen led me to a room where repair men were relaxing, and amid laughter they replaced the blown circuits. On another occasion, a taxi driver drove up half an hour after he had dropped me off at work bearing the credit card that I had left behind in his car. I have heard many similar examples of kindness.

For this reason, if someone comes up and asks if they can direct you anywhere, hesitate before replying. Except in the traditional tourist areas of a city, such queries are usually genuine and a hasty 'No!' may give offence where none was meant. Equally, they will be delighted if you make the first move and try to make contact with them.

Hot Tip: Enjoy Turkish Tea

One of the first ways of doing this is to accept a glass of tea, çay. Tea is served black with several lumps of sugar at the side of the glass and drunk in great quantities throughout the country. It may be offered in a kahve, literally 'coffee-house' (which as coffee is hardly drunk in them, is rather misnamed) or in banks, civil service offices or shops. Once you have had enough it is quite in order to refuse, because they themselves find they are drinking too much. (See cover illustration.)

At all times, Turkish people are careful to act according to the appropriate degree of respect, saygı. The respect an individual commands generally depends on their age, wealth, contacts and position they hold in their profession. Also, a father expects to receive respect from his children, wife, and relatives born in a later generation.

Failure to show the correct amount of respect is *ayıp*, shameful. Allowances are made for foreigners, but there are a few simple points which, once observed, make life easier.

Taking tea

Hot Tip: Do Not Interrupt!

Respect is shown to others particularly by allowing them to speak at length without interruption and looking attentive while they are speaking. The longer they speak, the more respect is given to them. It is very important that a person who feels entitled to respect is not contradicted in front of others. If a criticism is made, it may well be interpreted as a declaration of hostility.

As a guest, you are in a special category and entitled to respect. You will find that the people are invariably polite and anxious to agree with what you say. It is possible, therefore, that you may regard an appointment as being settled, and then find that no one turns up to meet you. If this happens, it is important not to get angry because failure to show up does not imply any dislike. Rather that, though unable to come, they wished to avoid the confrontation entailed in refusing, and chose the solution which caused the minimum of embarrassment for both sides.

Respect

The way to avoid misunderstandings is to think not of what is apparent on the surface but what is lying beneath. Every person in the room with you, whether in a village or in a business meeting in a town is acting according to the likely effect the discussion will have on them or their relations with others. Outsiders who are sympathetic to this way of thinking and careful to show respect where it is due will quickly be accepted.

Most people have a number of close friends, and an enormous number of acquaintances, *arkadaş*. Whenever a favour is required it is to these that they turn. If they need a seat in a bus when it is declared full, they phone up an *arkadaş* who works for the bus company and ask him or her to find a seat for them. If a hotel is full and a few more rooms need to be found then they turn to a fellow proprietor whom they have helped in the past. If they cannot help, someone who asks for advice they telephone an acquaintance and pass them along. Such exchanges of aid are an inescapable part of life in Turkey.

They do not just affect private life. Positions in the civil service, local and national government, and key roles within political parties are often allocated through personal contacts. Such ties are extremely significant in business, where having friends among the local officials and politicians may be vital in order to win contracts or see projects through.

Accordingly, it pays to be scrupulously polite and punctilious at all times in sending thank-you notes, occasional phone calls simply to inquire how people are getting along and regular visits. All these are deeply appreciated and you will not regret this effort when it becomes clear how warm a response it elicits. Indeed, the reputation of European people possess in Turkey of being cold and unemotional stems greatly from our not realizing just how important these little things are.

Overall the Turkish people are accustomed to paying far more attention to the other persons' feelings than is usual in Europe. They are courteous with strangers, spend endless trouble trying to make sure that they other person is comfortable, and are wonderful hosts. They regard time invested in human relationships well spent in itself, and will be desirous to avoid giving offence.

Hot Tip: Courtesy Counts

The extent of attention that a person is offered is an indication of their status, and they may find themselves disconcerted if they have not met with equal courtesy and time from their visitors. Turkish people always make allowances, but being as sensitive as possible to their culture brings enormous rewards in terms of the strength of friendships that may be formed.

NON-VERBAL COMMUNICATION

There are several distinct aspects to non-verbal communication that can be confusing at first. One of the most surprising to new arrivals is a habit of indicating 'no' by raising the eyebrows, clicking the tongue, tilting the head back or a combination of all three. If you have asked a question and not apparently had a response, look carefully to see whether the person you asked is raising his or her eyebrows. Sometimes, the signs can be almost imperceptible. Occasionally, too, they will indicate that something has long since happened (for example that the bus went some time ago) by a low, rising whistle accompanied by a waving rise of the right hand.

'Sometimes the signs can be almost imperceptible'

Physical contact between people of the same sex is closer than that we would be used to in Engklish-speaking countries – closer, perhaps, to that which is prevalent in Mediterranean countries. Friends may shake hands both when they meet and when they part. If they have not seen each other for some time, it would be usual for them to kiss each other on each cheek. People of the same sex may wander arm-in-arm in public. This also reflects itself in their interaction with babies, who may have their cheeks pulled affectionately and their hair ruffled, much to their surprise if they are used to less demonstrative interplay with adults.

FORMS OF ADDRESS

Just as in the West, Turkish names consist of a given name and a family name. In order to address a person respectfully in conversation add after the given name *bey* if a man and *hanım* if a woman. *Hanım* implies 'lady' rather than 'Miss' or 'Mrs'. There is no specific term for an unmarried woman. When writing, place *sayın* before the full name whether a man or a woman. So, to address a *Mehmet Şimşek* in conversation you would say *Mehmet bey*, when writing a letter to him you would say *Sayın* Mehmet Şimşek. To address a married woman *Ayşe Güçlü*, you would say *Ayşe hanım* when speaking but *Sayın* Ayşe Güçlü when writing. One of the reforms which has not become widespread, but is in use in banks and in civil service offices, is to place a prefix 'bay' or 'bayan' in front of the name, eg. *Bay Mehmet Şimşek*, and *Bayan Ayşe Güçlü*.

4

Food & Markets

'Meals are usually accompanied by alcohol'

Turkish cuisine is rightly renowned as one of the few distinct schools of cookery in the world, and at its best can rival any in variety and quality. The general standard of cooking is very much higher than in some Western countries, and all around large cities are little restaurants which have the dishes ready cooked and set out. This is very convenient, for one simply points to what one wants. The normal way of eating would be to take a main dish with rice, *pilav*, and perhaps yoghurt mixed with water, *ayran*, to drink. In these 'ready-meal' restaurants, there is no need to give a tip.

Be very polite with the proprietor because the bill may vary according to how much he likes you! I returned to a restaurant for the same particularly good soup several days running and each day as they began to get to know me better the price dropped by about 20 per cent until in the end I was paying less than half than on the first day.

Traditional Turkish cooking is giving way to 'fast-food' influences, and sadly there may be now occasions when you are disappointed with the quality offered. As a rule of thumb, avoid places, particularly in Istanbul, which appear to have given way to using large quantities of bright plastic in their décor. Be careful, too, of eating in hotels which appear to deal mostly in mass-tourism: these can offer travesties of Turkish cooking which bear a resemblance only in the name of the dishes. On the other hand, the ready food offered by street vendors is often much better than it looks, and though of course you should take elementary precautions as to how clean the stand appears, it may be very nice. Particularly look out for *simit*, fresh sesame-seed bread roundels which are usually sold hot by itinerant sellers. Their call '*Simiiiiiiitcheeee!*' echoes through the early evening in particular, as people leave their offices.

Baker's boy

When Turkish people wish to eat a snack, they often go to a *büfe*. These usually sell *tost*, which consists of bread pressed in a double-sided toasting machine and filled with cheese and pickle, or a piece of salami. They also make freshly-squeezed drinks from an abundance of fruit and vegetables: the best is perhaps orange juice (*portakal suyu*), closely rivaled by banana milk (which may be written as *muzlu süt* or *sütlü muz*) made by taking two bananas, a spoonful of honey and liquidising them into a pint of full-cream milk. They also may have an immense variety of other combinations, including fresh pomegranate (*nar*).

Hot Tip: Go for a Picnic!

In Ottoman Art, gardens often appear as an image of heaven. The love of gardens has remained, and in the summer picnics in orchards and beauty spots are very popular. Picnics are always held in a very leisurely fashion and are a delightful way to experience Turkish life. The food will be absolutely fresh. There will be no pork, which is forbidden by the Koran, but plenty of yoghurt, honey, bread, salad, steak and fruit.

Turkish people also enjoy eating outdoors in towns. Most restaurants have a garden in which diners may continue to sit after it gets dark. Usually a meal begins with starters, *meze*. These may be either cold or hot. Among cold starters are yoghurt, olives, stuffed peppers, pureed aubergine, goat's and sheep's cheese and many varieties of salad. Among hot starters most common are various sautéed meats, sea food dishes (particularly squid or octopus) and *börek*, pastry stuffed with cheese, meat, spinach, or mushroom. After this comes the main course, usually roasted or grilled fish or meat, often served with rice, tomato and salads. All savoury food is accompanied by bread. The sweet may consist of pastries soaked in syrup, or fruit. Coffee comes black, in small cups. If you wish it plain, you may ask for *sade*, if with sugar, *şekerli*.

Such a rich and varied meal is quite normal. The meal may well last from the early evening until late at night. In your conversation it is better not to raise problems of ethnic minorities, religion or politics in Turkey until you know your hosts well. They, however, may ask you detailed questions on contemporary affairs, sport, Western governments, theory of democracy, religion, law, the European Union and the way Turkey is regarded by the West. This last is a very sensitive topic, and you may need to reassure your hosts several times of the goodwill your country holds for them.

Turkish restaurant

DRINK

Meals in the evening are often accompanied by alcohol. This is a useful way to understand the attitude of your hosts to religion. Increasingly, those who are very pro-Islam are refusing to drink or to serve drink at public functions, so if your contact is with a local municipality, a construction company or an institution or trust which has religious/political leanings or connections with the former *Refah* (Welfare) party they are unlikely to serve alcohol. If drink is served, it is likely to include the national drink *rakı*, a strong spirit somewhat similar to ouzo, which is mixed with water until it turns cloudy. Beer is drunk all over Turkey. Wine tends to be found only in the urban areas. It is made locally and is quite palatable. In whatever social milieu, it is regarded as shameful to be drunk.

Hot Tip: Watch the Beer!

Be careful therefore of the beer: it is much stronger than most Western brews and only a few bottles on a hot day can produce very powerful results.

PAYMENT

If you have just arrived in Turkey, and are with Turkish hosts, it would be quite wrong for you to pay for the meal. If you have had time to get to know the people with whom you are dining, it may be possible to offer to pay if you are extremely tactful. If they refuse, then a possible solution is to pay the waiter discreetly in such a way that your actions are not apparent to the rest of the company. This is an established custom, and the waiter will realize what you are doing. Service is included in the bill, but on top of this in the more expensive restaurants it is normal to add between five and ten per cent (always in cash) for the waiter.

Lira

MONEY

The Turkish unit of currency is the Lira (TL). In Spring 1999, the Lira was approximately 500,000 to the pound, and 300,000 to the dollar. Inflation (at the time of writing) is high, at least sixty-five per cent a year, and has been consistently higher than this in the past.

Hot Tip: Change Money on Arrival

Visitors are advised to wait until their arrival in Turkey before changing money, and then in small quantities.

Sums sufficient for all personal expenditure are freely available in a number of different ways: automatic cash dispensers are ubiquitous throughout the country, certainly in all provincial centres (*il*) and in nearly all sub-provincial centres (*ilçe*). These take visa, and a range of other plastic cards. A multitude of private exchange bureaux have opened up. Unlike other European countries, these often take no commission at all, gaining their profit through the 'spread' between buying and selling.

They can be very reasonable, though, as always, rates should be checked. Most hotels will change money (often at rather poor rates) and banks still accept euro-cheques and travellers cheques. As the rise of plastic cards continues, these last two are fast losing their attraction for banks, and they should no longer be considered the prime means of obtaining cash.

SHOPPING

Turkey's astonishing economic transformation has resulted in a huge boom in fashion items. Overseas companies have been quick to catch on also, and Marks & Spencer's recent opening in Istanbul (rumour has it that they sold off their entire stock in one day's trading) is typical of the way that a society is willingly transforming itself into a major player in the world's consumer markets. Turkey has also consistently shown itself to be in the forefront of computer software adoption, and is enthusiastically embracing internet technology.

All this means that almost anything available in the West can also be found in Turkey. Nevertheless, there are still traces remaining of a distinction that used to be more important: goods are often found in two versions: one made locally (*yerli*) and the other imported (*ithal*). Imported goods are substantially more expensive than local ones, so when buying anything be careful that you are paying the appropriate price.

The quality of locally-made products varies. Broadly speaking, electrical goods and common pharmaceuticals are of a reasonable quality; textiles, though uneven, may be very fine indeed. Turkish stationary used to be very poor but is fast getting better, particularly in the main cities. Turkish cheeses and wines are often very good. Local vodka (*vodka*), gin (*cin*) or cognac (*konyak*) made under the government monopoly are not recommended and possibly even harmful.

Even the quality of imported goods may vary; with well-known internationals appearing to dump slightly less high quality products on the market, but still use their brand name. I was caught like this with razor blades, and it might still be a good idea to bring such absolutely essential personal effects with one, though this should continue to become increasingly less necessary.

Turkey has a wide selection of reasonably-priced traditional goods and crafts. Leather goods, carpets, rugs, copperware and onyx are all made to a high standard. There are several places to buy them. Sometimes a particular town specializes in one particular product. Alternatively, a variety of traditional crafts are sold through outlets administered by the Ministry of Tourism in most large cities and tourist towns.

Hot Tip: Museum Shops are Good, and Bazaars are Fun!

Look out for the museum shops. Their prices are often fixed by an association in support of the museum, and extremely reasonable. This is probably the surest way to gain value for money as both quality and price are controlled. In spite of this, the most enjoyable place to buy goods is in a bazaar, although this means being prepared to bargain to obtain a good price.

BARGAINING

The price of products made under government monopoly are not negotiable. These include cigarettes and alcohol. In most modern shops the price of goods is clearly marked and bargaining may not be acceptable, though no offence will be taken should you ask politely whether there is any room for manoeuvre. In the markets and covered bazaars bargaining is the norm. Here, it cannot be stated too forcefully that there is no necessary connection between the worth of the goods offered and the price demanded. Thus, even if you offer half the quoted amount you still may be offering many times more than the fair price. In order to escape this problem it is a good idea to wait until you have a feel of the going rates.

Hot Tip: Do Not be Hurried!

At all times, do not be hurried by the vendor, do not be afraid to refuse to buy if you feel the price is still too high, and have a look at the produce of several sellers before buying anything.

Covered bazaar, Istanbul

Finally, a warning or two: when buying carpets (and they are very attractive) it is safer not to use a visa card unless the owner can clearly be trusted. Very rarely, visa slips have been changed after the purchase to the buyer's disadvantage. The covered bazaar in Istanbul, though absolutely spectacular is perhaps a very inadvisable place to purchase souvenirs unless with a close Turkish friend.

Hot Tip: Remember, the Tour Guide Gets a Commission

Do not forget that tour guides obtain a commission from any shop-keeper that they have introduced you to. This may be as high as 30 per cent. For this reason, though your guide may be scrupulously honest, bear in mind that he is also an interested party and probably not in a position to give neutral advice as to the beauty and age of the piece you are admiring!

5

Festivals & Ceremonies

Topkapı Palace interior

As in other countries, the year is broken up into a series of public holidays some of which are derived from religious ceremonies, whilst others mark important dates in the nation's history. In particular, 23 April marks the founding of the Grand National Assembly – 30 August, victory day in the War of Independence, and 29 October the declaration of the Republic. On these three days, as you would expect, banks and civil service offices are closed. On these days, too, there may be civil rituals and military parades throughout the country, and a large procession in Ankara televised throughout the country.

New Year's day is also a bank holiday which has grown enormously in commercial importance in recent years. A traditional new year's ball in the Ankara Palas, an event that Atatürk used to enjoy, has recently been resurrected, whilst shops may have greenery, even trees as part of their festive decorations. Many families eat roast turkey on that day (known locally as *hindi*), and it is the done thing to send small greetings cards to friends and relatives with the season's compliments. Whilst Turkish friends will not really expect to receive a Christmas card, they appreciate a greeting sent for the New Year, and you may receive one from them.

Leaving aside these secular holidays, the most important festivals for the majority of the population, particularly in the villages, are based on the religious calendar. As in Christianity, peoples' knowledge of some of these aspects of theology may not be very strong, and different groups may celebrate to a different extent. Nevertheless, the month-long Ramadan, *Ramazan*, and the Feast of Sacrifice (*Kurban bayramı*) that follows two months and ten days after this are widely respected.

The Feast of Sacrifice is marked by three days' public holiday, whilst the end of the Ramadan by one day's holiday, known as the Sugar Bayram, *Şeker Bayramı*. Their timing varies according to the lunar calendar, and as they move each year they may come to coincide with the secular public holidays. In this case, the days are put together and celebrated accumulatively. It is possible that everything may stay closed for a week, particularly as it is quite normal for the Prime Minister to declare an extra day or half-day's holiday if by doing so the weekend may be become part of the bank holiday.

During Ramadan believers fast during the hours of daylight. From dawn until sunset they do not drink, eat or smoke. Normal office hours are worked, although this is sometimes a matter of controversy among religious activists. Most people are tolerant of a foreigner's normal habits, but it puts great strain on those who are fasting if others eat in front of them. During this period, restaurants are often screened so that they cannot be seen from the street, and some may be closed during the day.

Hot Tip: Respect for Ramadan

Throughout Ramadan, try to avoid eating in public places. During the day, those who are fasting attempt to do as little as possible so as to conserve energy. It is not wise to take a taxi or a bus just before the end of the fast as people are hurrying to reach their destination for the break of fast. If it is hot weather be more than usually careful in traffic, because tempers are particularly short during that period when the head is aching with hunger, and the throat swollen with thirst.

During Ramadan mosques suspend lights from their minarets, and the television broadcasts soothing music and recitals from the Koran. Ministers and even the Prime Minister have in recent years used the break of fast as sun sets, known as *iftar*, to provide special celebratory meals for invited guests, which are widely followed and reported in the press. Likewise, most other people invite each other to their houses to eat the spicy bread, special milky puddings, *pide* and soup that are only found during that month.

It is usual to wake up just before daybreak to eat a large breakfast. In many areas, people are woken up by the sound of a lone (but loud) drummer hailing before day break to wake people up before sunrise so that they may eat in good time before light. Do not be surprised should you find a knock on your door by the drummer at the end of the month asking for a tip. At that point, those people who have decided not to fast have been tempted to say what they think of a month of being woken up before daybreak, but it is courteous to leave any complaints to the local people (who will know much better how to do so), and offer a small amount, perhaps £2-3 ($3-5) or so to the drummer, with good grace.

there are 40 million sheep in Turkey

KURBAN BAYRAMI (Feast of Sacrifice)

On the Feast of Sacrifice, traditionally all families who could afford to do so sacrifice. Usually, a sheep is chosen, but it may also be a larger beast or even a camel. The festival is a time for reconciliation, for families to gather together. A wealthy person may distribute meat from the sacrifice to those poorer than themselves, and take the opportunity to distribute alms. The state requires that the pelts from the beasts are given to the Turkish Air Foundation, a charitable trust that supports the air force, who though they may keep a proportion of the money so gained, dispose of the rest to several other recognized charities. This custom originated in the days when Turkey was much poorer, and the money from them was no doubt extremely useful. Today, it is regarded as a useful way to impede the flow of donations to fundamentalist organizations who otherwise might benefit from the sale of the skins.

LIFE-CYCLES

Within the individual progression from birth, adulthood and death, birthdays are given less importance than in the West. The two most important ceremonies are for boys' circumcision, *sünnet*, and for both sexes, marriage. Circumcision may take place at any age between about three and thirteen. If the boy is still young, then it is the tradition to dress him up in a brightly-coloured soldiers' uniform, with a *fez* and hold a party celebrating the happy event. A man who has made his fortune may sometimes help those less fortunate by paying for their circumcision ceremonies through a charitable foundation, *vakıf*.

Marriage is rather more elaborate. A civil marriage became obligatory during the Republic. This only takes a few minutes, and is often supplemented in villages with festivals that may last as long as three days. Traditionally, in villages, the bride moves to the house of her groom; both houses hold a series of meals, and there may be dancing and drinking. In villages in central and Western Anatolia, dance music is usually supplied by a pair of musicians who play a drum and pipe, *davul* and *zurna*. The dances are lively, vary according to region, and well worth joining in with if the opportunity occurs.

In the cities, where it is more difficult to find areas where people might come together to celebrate, you can now find large halls, known as wedding saloons, which may be rented just for the afternoon. Unless the person organizing the wedding is very rich, no food will be provided. Indeed, it is often the case that the more prominent guests are expected to walk forward to pin money onto the bride's dress. This rather obligatory form of present-giving make peoples' presence at these events decidedly ambivalent. Yet, people feel that they should go, even if only because they would also like a good crowd when it is their turn to arrange their children's marriages, and their absence may be quietly noted.

People with more money may instead hold a wedding ceremony in a hotel, and the Hilton, Sheraton and other establishments cater for them in different ways. At one I attended, the religious infuence was very slight. Rather, the bare civil rite was pepped up by the couple being placed on a podium, and to the sound of repeated drum music, six flunkies dressed in togas and holding torches came into the room, surrounding them as they performed their vows. This institutionalized five-star pagan hospitality seemed to go down very well.

SAINTS & TOMBS

Hot Tip: Importance of Tomb-visiting

An interesting characteristic of Turkish Islam is for people, both men and women, to make a vow at the tomb of a saint. Such tomb-visiting is prevalent all over Turkey.

Izmir: decorative relief end of Ⓒ17

Whilst one of the first Republican reforms was to ban tomb-visiting, it quickly became clear that this was a measure too far. In 1950, worship at many of the more important tombs was officially permitted once again. Now, large tombs such as at Eyüp or at the Süleymaniye complexes, both in Istanbul, are very popular with men and women alike.

When visiting tombs, the visiting supplicant makes their prayer in the form of a wish and vow, known as *adak*: thus, should God grant the following favour (such as a son returning safely from military conscription, passing exams safely), then they will perform the following task out of gratitude. Usually, the penance is in the form of making a contribution to a pious charity, or offering a sacrifice. Exceptionally, it may be more grand, such as building a new mosque.

Tombs may also be used to cure or assist those with physical ailments. These smaller tombs are found all over the countryside and form an important part of local religious customs. Different tombs may be regarded as particularly efficacious for different purposes: one may be known for curing malaria, another against mental illness, another for those who wish to have a child and so on. Often, a mother will bring a portion of the sick person's clothing and leave it at the tomb, or they may tie a little ribbon on the trees nearby.

The efficacy of the tombs is said to come through their being the resting place of a person, usually a male, who is said to have been favoured by God with a special sign of their worth. In Turkey, for a living person to make such a claim is now against the law, as are the organizations, brotherhoods, *tarikat*, that tend to form round such claimants and their descendants all over the Islamic world. Though still illegal, such brotherhoods are in fact largely tolerated. For the visitor, this tolerance is particularly important in that two of the largest and oldest brotherhoods, the Mevlevi, and the Bektashı hold annual festivals, and possess spectacular tomb complexes that are well-maintained today.

THE MEVLEVI

The Mevlevi were formed in Konya during the time of the Seljuks. Their founder, Celalettin Rumi is known for a long corpus of mystical writing, parts of which have often been translated into English. Their religious philosophy is based on the exploration of the inner self, and is celebrated in a distinctive whirling dance accompanied by a flute known as the *ney*.

Their centre, known as the Mevlana, which contains the tomb of their founder, is now a museum in Konya. Visited by more than a million people a year, it is popular with tourists and locals alike. Though to proselytize their movement is forbidden, for one week a year, the Mevleric perform their dance as a tourist attraction, with the performers paid by the state. Very popular still, it is possible to obtain specific tours to Turkey just to go to this week of performances. The event is prefaced by speeches, but it is important to be patient as the wait to see the entrancing and delicate movements is certainly worth it. Recently, a Mevlevi lodge in Istanbul appears to have been reformed, and it is possible to see performances there also.

Eastern Black Sea folk dance

THE BEKTASHI

The centre of the Bektashi brotherhood lies at the town of Haci-Bektaş in Kırşehir province, in the centre of Anatolia. The Bektashi are famed for their particularly esoteric form of mystical contemplation, one that takes them very close to the position reached by the Persian Hafiz, with his images of the eternal love of a nightingale for a rose that can never be grasped.

Whilst they previously had many adherents in the cities, their importance in the Republic results from Haci-Bektash being the patron saint of nearly all the Alevi, a heterodox minority that consists of about twenty per cent of Turkey's population. The Alevi are not well known: partly this is because of their preferring to keep their ceremonies secret. Recently, however, they are becoming more conscious of their culture.

Hot Tip: August Festival

Each year there is a sizeable festival in Kırşehir during the month of August, at which Alevi come from all over Turkey to display their distinctive music, dance and discuss their customs in learned seminars.

Finally, it is worth noting that there are also local festivals, often based on produce. It is worthwhile inquiring at a local tourist office to find out whether there are any planned. Among the things celebrated are Afyon cream (similar to English Devon clotted cream), and melons. Usually, these celebrations include displays of folklore or other customs and last for two or three days. Thus, there may be oiled wrestling, displays of *jirit* (a highly skilled jousting display, wherein two teams on horseback attempt to strike their opponents with blunted javelins), traditional dancing and so on.

There may also be music or poetry competitions between minstrels. These last may reach an exceptional standard. If at a small town or country festival, *şenlik*, look out for the moment in the proceedings whereby a man may become 'festival king' by offering the greatest sum of money to a charity, the amount decided in a public auction against his rivals. As the figures become higher and higher, the tension can become enthralling.

6

Out & About

Seljuk Fortress, Alanya

Anywhere in Turkey, finding a place to stay is rarely a problem. Istanbul has several hotels of international standard, the most established being the Hilton (Cumhuriyet Caddesi, Harbiye). More modern are the Sheraton (Taksim Parkı, Taksim) and the Etap Istanbul (Meşrutiyet Cadde-si). The Pera Palas hotel, (Meşrutiyet Caddesi 98-100), built to celebrate the coming of the Orient

Express has the most atmosphere. All these hotels are found above Pera, in the modern part of the city.

Cheaper establishments of vastly differing standards are situated across the Golden Horn, close by the Blue Mosque. Some are acceptable and pleasantly furnished (though it is always wise to check the plumbing facilities), others are very basic. There are several youth hostels in this area, which should be treated with some caution, as in spite of the official-sounding name they are privately run and often not up to scratch.

The pattern is similar for other large cities. Ankara, which previously lacked large hotels, now has two which are very attractive: the Hilton and the Sheraton, both in Kavaklıdere. Lower-priced hotels are situated in Ulus, the heart of the old quarter. The older hotels in Ulus are a good introduction to the facilities to be expected outside the tourist areas.

Hot Tip: If You Choose a Local Hotel. . .

Almost all towns have hotels, usually situated near the market square, but they cater mainly for Turkish people. Rooms are sparsely furnished, often with no more than a bed in them. Toilets are likely to be the squat-style. However, the service is invariably cheerful and friendly and the bed usually comfortable.

TRAVELLING

For many people, the beauty of visiting Turkey is the Mediterranean coast, with its long beaches and plethora of archaeological remains. Other areas are equally interesting. Winter sports are expanding quickly, whilst there are an increasing number of specialist tours catering for minority interests such as trekking or riding. Turkish people themselves love to travel, and many families now possess a summer-house or *yazlık* on the coast to which they 'escape' as quickly as they can in high summer.

Istanbul

Istanbul remains a focal point for many of the population. Most visitors at some point in their stay make a trip to this fascinating city. Here, too, signs of change are to be found everywhere. The

Turkish people have a taste for good singing, eating, for dressing well, for enjoying themselves which is accompanying their rising standard of living. Restaurants, night clubs, venues for music, theatre and cinema are opening rapidly. Where Istanbul was once a large, sprawling metropolis whose entertainment facilities lagged behind its importance as a tourist and international business destination, now it is developing a dynamic, a sensuosity, which has restored it to being an international fashionable attraction in its own right.

Nevertheless, walking around the city is still an extraordinary experience, giving one a sense of how life must have been during the era of the Ottoman Empire, with its sultans, harems, lavish palaces and huge mosques. Alongside this lies the evidence of the city's Byzantine past, in particular the church of Holy Wisdom, Haghia Sofia, the frescoes of St Saviour in Chora and the remains of the Hippodrome, where the chariot races used to be disrupted by rioting.

The best way to get to know the city is by a combination of walking and using different forms of public transport. The old city lies on a small peninsular between the Bosphorus and the Golden Horn. The Sultan's Palace, Topkapı Sarayı, the covered bazaar, Kapalı Çarşısı, the Blue Mosque, Sultan Ahmet, and most of the Byzantine remains are situated there. On the other side of the Golden Horn are the old merchants' quarters and the modern part of the city. Across the Bosphorus is a splinter part of the city which is linked by frequent ferry crossings. The visitor will probably begin in the old quarter of the city and then walk down to Galata Bridge, across the Golden Horn and along İstiklal Avenue to Taksim Square, the heart of the modern city.

Hot Tip: A Woman's Best Response

The streets of Istanbul are quite peaceful, and assault is uncommon. Unfortunately, though men may look around all day without experiencing the slightest discourtesy, women on their own tend to be harangued in a most unpleasant way. *Defol!* 'Clear off!' said very firmly is the most likely word to achieve results.

As well as normal taxis there are collective taxis, *dolmuş. Dolmuş* literally means 'stuffed' and, as this implies, they set off when all the places are taken. The routes and fares are fixed by the municipality. Each person passes their fare to the driver by means of the person in front so it is quite likely that someone will tap you on the shoulder and wave money under your nose. In that case, tap the person in front of you on the shoulder and pass the money on. Any change will be passed back by the passengers in the same way. There are buses, but they are usually rather crowded and but for certain urban bus clearways in Istanbul, not recommended.

One of the most enjoyable aspects of wandering around the city is to see the wealth of street traders. boot-blacks are everywhere. They put a shine on shoes but their materials are not to be trusted. In particular avoid them in the rainy season for the base they use (which they often tint according to the colour of the shoe) often turns white when wet.

. . . a synthesis between the Muslim and Western worlds

TRAVELLING IN ANATOLIA

Anatolia is a vast land mass, high plains alternate with steep valleys and rapid changes in micro-climate. Even a week of simply travelling around more or less at random will provide a store of rich impressions of quite unique landscapes and changing ways of life. Whilst it is easy to rent a car, the best way to see all this is to travel by coach. Local driving is often very daring, and not always predictable. Coaches, however, are cheap, ultra-modern and reliable.

Recently, smoking (a bane of generations of travellers in Anatolia) has been banned on coaches as part of a general crackdown on smoking in public places. There is a concession in that drivers are allowed to smoke as a way of keeping themselves awake, so do not be surprised if you see them light-up.

There are many different coach companies. Between large cities, the most famous are *Varan*, *Kamil Koç* and *Ulusoy*. Most towns have a terminal, however, and it is easiest simply to go to buy a ticket when you need one. At the terminal, take care not to be pressurized into buying a ticket before checking when the bus goes and what route it runs on. The terminals are crowded and hot, and it is easy to loose one's temper. It is better to remain calm until it seems absolutely necessary to state one's case more firmly.

Hot Tip: Never Offer Physical Violence

Never offer physical violence; if a little fuss does not produce the desired result, the likelihood is that what you want really is not possible.

It is also possible to travel by train and plane. There is a good network of internal flights, operated until recently by Turkish Airways, though now some routes have been opened up to competition. This means that travel between Istanbul, Ankara, Izmir, Bodrum and Antalya (among others) is easily achievable by air. It is probably safer to take the state company rather than the private companies, whose safety record is not as high as it might be. Road travel is so quick between towns (particularly between Istanbul and Ankara) that it is not always much quicker to take the plane, though it may offer variety.

Train travel, in contrast, is leisurely, and the rolling stock often old. Nevertheless, it can be pleasant. The night-train between Istanbul and Ankara is a part of life in Anatolia. Indeed, to drink a glass of *rakı* in the restaurant car, watching the steppe go by before retiring to a sleeper, then to wake up in the imposing Haydarpaşal station in Istanbul and breakfast in the little restaurant there with its coloured tiles, is one of the joys of travel in Turkey. Do not, however, do this before a morning *rendezvous*. The train might be on time, but it equally likely might not.

Provincial travel provides a good opportunity to see plenty of historic architecture. Traditionally, the Ottomans built their town houses out of wood. Frequent fires, and later rapid development means that the cities (with the exception of Istanbul) have almost all come to resemble each other: newly-built concrete apartments that differ in the space and the luxury available to their occupants but are architecturally similar. Villages and smaller towns have partly taken this path, but it is possible to see still an immense variety of building styles.

In Amasya, for example (about three hours on the coach from Ankara), there is a famous row of wooden houses along a wide river that runs through the centre of the city. They are well-preserved and one has been made into a museum. In Capadoccia, where the rock is soft, it is possible to see both beautiful stone houses, and also cave villages. Caves were often popular in this region because they are easy to keep at a constant temperature in both winter and summer. Today, cave settlements are largely abandoned, though several have been made into open-air museums, and one even, a hotel.

THE COUNTRYSIDE

Slightly less than half of Turkey's population lives in the countryside and of the town-dwellers may have only recently migrated to the urban areas. People will tell you how proud they are of their village, claiming that its water is clean, the setting beautiful and the hospitality second to none. Indeed, it is true that if you go to a village it is likely that you will be pressed to eat, drink and even to stay the night. Village life is more formal than in the town, so that if you accept you will find the rules of showing respect to elders and to guests are especially marked.

Hot Tip: Women and Village Etiquette

Do not be surprised if you see only men. Village life has retained the traditional separation between the sexes, a custom that is now rare in cities. Women may enter only briefly to wish you welcome. The men of the visiting party should take care not to address a woman directly, nor to look too long at them. Of course, it would be folly to make a pass at a village woman, and likely to result in violence. Women visitors have rather more choice. They may stay with the men as guests, or depart with the village women to their quarters.

On leaving, do not offer money, for this shames the village's hospitality. If you have in your bag a few pieces of good quality, brightly-coloured cloth then the women would appreciate this as a gift. An easier way to reciprocate is to take photographs and send them to the village. Men usually do not mind being photographed. Village women will probably be delighted but the only tactful method is for the women of the visiting party to take photographs when there are no males present. Be careful only to take obviously harmless pictures, for example, of village life, and of course never near borders or military establishments.

Hot Tip: Shoes Off!

On entering a house anywhere in Turkey, it is normal to take off one's shoes. The host will usually offer slippers to wear whilst in their home. In villages, the Islamic greeting *selamunaleykum*, 'peace by with you!', is customary. If someone has said *selam* to you, it is extremely impolite not to return it with the appropriate reply, *aleykumselam*, 'peace be upon you!' In the city, you may prefer to initiate a greeting with the more secular *merhaba*!, Hello!

At home

ON BEING INVITED TO STAY

If you are in Turkey for any length of time, it is likely that you will be invited to stay in someone's home. Such generosity is found throughout Turkey, among rich and poor. Whilst deciding whether to accept there are some pros and cons to consider.

Traditionally, a guest has to be very closely looked after, their wishes anticipated and all their needs attended to. The invitation may be made more from a desire to please or out of a feeling of duty, than actually wanting to take on the very considerable burden of being a host.

A guest also has obligations. In accepting the invitation you are placing yourself under the responsibility of the hosts, and should not go against their wishes whilst staying with them. There is a saying which illustrates this, *ev sahibı sultandır!*, the host is sultan!

It is a point of honour that guests should not spend any money. If you find offers to pay are repeatedly refused, do not persist. Where we should try to recompense a host by reciprocating fairly quickly, for example, when buying drinks, usually they would do so over a far longer period. According to their rules, first the host must have the chance to display his or her generosity, and only later does the guest attempt to repay. It would be quite acceptable to send a gift after returning home, or on a subsequent visit to bring presents with you. If you wish to do something whilst you are still there, it is quite acceptable to buy flowers, which are plentiful and deeply loved throughout Turkey. Sweet cakes such as *baklava*, or chocolate for the children are also possibilities.

To have guests is a way of increasing one's status; thus you may receive other invitations from your host's neighbours or business associates. If you genuinely wish to stay in a different home it is better to do so on your next visit, so as not to insult your present host.

A town family group

GREETINGS

As you enter a strange house be prepared for the greeting *'Hoş geldiniz!'*, 'Welcome!' The correct reply is *'Hoş bulduk!'*, 'Well-found!' As each new person comes into the room he or she will repeat the greeting and shake your hand. If a person is much younger than you he or she may kiss your hand and press it to their forehead. If the new arrival is an elderly man then it is polite to stand up for him.

On parting, those leaving say '*Allaha ismarla-dık*', 'We have consigned ourselves to God', or more simply '*İyi günler*', 'Good-day'. Those not leaving respond '*Güle güle*', 'Go laughingly'. Note that the party leaving speaks first, and the 'go smilingly' is a reply to their farewell. If, as you are leaving, you repeat your 'good day' then those staying will repeat 'go smilingly' and you may find yourself in a continuous cycle of goodbyes.

Hot Tip: Who Goes First

In a town, and with a woman who appears Westernized, then a man should step back to allow her through first. If in a village, or if the woman is wearing a headscarf, then the man must step through the door before the woman. This is important because in many villages a woman is brought up never to cross a man's path on the grounds that it brings bad luck, *uğur kesme*. It may cause acute embarrassment if a man insists that the woman enters before him.

7

Business Matters

Istanbul hotel

Turks work from Mondays to Fridays, usually starting at nine in the morning and working until five or six at night. Lunch is taken around midday. Most people take their annual holidays during the hottest part of the year in July and August. The holiday period is not a favourable time to conduct business nor are the first few days of Ramadan.

The business centre of Turkey is Istanbul, and the industrial belt runs from Istanbul along the coast down through Izmit and into the western part of Anatolia. However, Ankara is also an important centre, and one of the most interesting phenomenon of recent years is the way other large cities (such as Gaziantep in the south-east or Bursa nearer Istanbul) have grown sufficiently confident to run very significant economic transactions on their own behalf, largely independently of the national scene.

The great success of the Turkish economic programme is evident. Textile and clothing, communications, and financial services are buoyant. The latest cars, many manufactured in Turkey to the latest standards, are everywhere. The national airline, *Türk Hava Yolları*, repeatedly and proudly publicises the fact that their fleet of planes is amongst the youngest in the world. There are many more commercial television channels than in most European countries, with many towns, even some with a population of only 50,000, possessing more than one local channel. National television stations, sustained on a diet of pop music, chat shows and news (varying slightly according to the political approach of the proprietor) are available on cable and satellite throughout Anatolia, and their vigour in turn forces the state channels to look to their laurels.

The combination of a quickly growing population with an equally quickly growing economy presents a very attractive scenario for those contemplating doing business in Turkey. Whilst this is not mistaken, there are some points to bear in mind. The state bureaucracy has not kept up with this growing change. At the outset of the Republic, economic and social development was largely channelled through the state, who were responsible for whole sectors, including government monopolies in steel, tobacco, drink and sugar. These have partly been superseded by the growth of the private sector, and a drive toward privatization begun by the late President Özal, and continued by his successors.

Privatization has not been as complete as first envisaged. The bureaucracy remains overmanned poorly paid, often inefficient, and hampered by political appointments, decisions are accorded on the basis of local or personal expediency.

Hot Tip: Intricate Regulations Are a Problem

Intricate rules governing taxation, permits, planning and procedure are so complicated that Turkish people themselves sometimes feel obliged to complain about them.

This is the great challenge facing the visitor to Turkey. On the one hand they have the opportunity to experience a fast-moving private sector, and an intense lively charming population who work and play hard. Indeed, one of the great pleasures of businessmen from overseas working in Turkey is that, accustomed only to eking out market share in saturated markets, they learn a host of new skills in catering for expanding demand. On the other, they must learn to deal with a government service that, whatever its faults, still has the power to make the rules of the country. The law of the land is theirs but wealth generation is the private sector's. The person who learns how to move between these two extremes will be doing very well indeed.

Tram system in downtown Istanbul

When establishing links, bear in mind that business transactions are seen as partly to do with finance and partly to do with building up a relationship over a number of years. If a Turkish firm buys equipment from you, they may feel that they have the right to expect you to take on some trainees the following year. Or they may ask you to bring some special piece of equipment or tool with you next time you come to Turkey. If negotiations are not going well, think in terms of the possibilities of such contact in the future that you are offering the Turkish side.

It helps enormously to have letters of introduction, from a person who is familiar to those you are introducing yourself to. If you have a particular purpose you should have letters from someone in an official position explaining your background and reason for being in Turkey. These should have as many large, official-looking stamps as possible. If you wish to get something done the very worst way to go about it is to approach the person concerned with no more than a passport to introduce yourself.

There are complex regulations concerning the amount of property a foreigner may own in Turkey, and equally complex regulations governing the tariffs on importing and exporting, though the situation is changing quite quickly as a result of the customs union. The best way to overcome these is to develop close ties with a local individual or firm and ask them to explain the step to take in each case. The nearest Turkish Embassy may be able to help with specific queries, or alternatively your Embassy in Ankara.

The European Commission web-page has a useful number of documents on the question of Turkey and the Customs Union (use the general 'search' facility from the home page), but they seem generally to prefer that enquiries in the first instance be channelled through an office in the host country. Within the European Union, most member states possess designated offices, whilst the Union itself has representatives in many capitals, including Ankara.

Business cards are very widely used. Be punctual for business appointments; occasionally it happens that the visitor, anxious to be as relaxed as the locals, arrives half an hour late whilst the host, anxious not to appear inefficient turns up exactly on time.

APPEARANCE

Dress should be smart; Turkish businessmen and civil servants always dress in a suit and tie or its ladies' equivalent. Clothes can be bought locally but extreme care should be taken as to the quality of the garment. One cannot trust a particular shop because each seems to be supplied by a number of sources which may vary from week to week.

When having a haircut, allow ample time, because it is a mark of respect to the client for the hairdresser to be fastidious concerning the final result. Shaving, which is almost entirely done with a cut-throat razor, takes more than half an hour and several glasses of tea. It is appropriate to leave a tip of about ten per cent for the man who did the cutting and rather less for the boy who takes the coat.

'Dress should be smart'

CONTRACTS, THE LAW & COMPLETION

Over the last decades, foreign investment in Turkey has increased steadily. However, the smallest projects to the very largest, such as that to install natural gas in Ankara, or a sewage system in Izmir, have occasionally encountered misunderstandings. Many of these appear to hinge around a different interpretation of contractual agreements.

There are several reasons for this. First, we tend to think that when an arrangement has been proposed it implies that the necessary work behind the scenes has already been achieved. In Turkey this is not always the case. Sometimes, the offer is an indication of interest in principle. If so, it is only *after* the contract is signed that the important work to ensure that the project will go ahead is actually achieved. This is significant in small firms, where there may be a question of consultation with the owner or other partner. It is even more so in large infrastructure projects where the financial and political complications that are attendant upon the project's success are so complex that the people who are doing the negotiations may themselves not see the way through them.

How can these difficulties be averted? The first thing to say is that there are very many firms successfully conducting business in Turkey. The most successful of these appear to be ready to be flexible. They appear to be prepared to put an immense amount of effort into developing personal relations and do not take it for granted that their business culture is the same as their hosts. They appear to be patient, and sympathetic to the multiple pressures and strains that the people on the Turkish side will no doubt be experiencing. Pragmatically, money should only be committed to a project when it is absolutely sure that everything is ready on the other side: working across cultures really does take that little bit of extra time to ensure everything is clearly understood.

8

Useful Phrases & Vocabulary

Street signs

Turkish has been written in the Roman alphabet since the early years of the republic. It is regular and not at all linked to Arabic, though there are loan words. The biggest obstacle at the beginning is the strange vocabulary, followed closely by a rather unusual grammar. The key idea is that the root, a verb or noun, does not change and inflexions are added to it to express case, tense or person. This may seem a little difficult to get used to, but once grasped almost any situation can be expressed simply and precisely. Thus *gelmek* = to come; *-mek* is the usual infinitive ending. To say 'I am coming' one takes the stem *gel* and adds to this the sign for the present tense *iyor* and that of the first person singular -m to make *geliyorum*. Complicated constructions are outside the scope of this book, but it is worth stressing that the friendly response from the people on whom one tries out one's efforts amply repays the trouble taken in learning.

Language need not be an insurmountable barrier. It is easy to pick up a few words of Turkish, sufficient at least to show you friendly intent, and there are enough English speakers in the major centres who could deal with a serious problem. If need be, useful words are *merhaba*, hello; *evet*, yes; *hayır*, no; *teşekkür ederim*, thank you. A simpler way of saying thank-you is *sağ ol!* Health be! An absolutely necessary word is 'Yok!' Yok is used everywhere to signify none, not any, or an emphatic no!

PRONOUNCING THE LANGUAGE

The Turkish language is written in Roman script, and words are pronounced just as they would be in English with the following exceptions.

ı said as is the 'o' in women;

ç said as is the 'ch' in church;
c said as is the 'j' in jam;
o said as is the 'eu' in the French veut
ş said as is the 'sh' in wish;
ğ said as is the 'y' in yellow, lengthens the
   preceding vowel'
ü said as is the 'u' in the French rue

Turkish never runs two consonants together, thus *kütüphane*, library, is pronounced kütüp-hane, with a clearly marked 'h'.

POLITE WORDS AND PHRASES

Merhaba	hello
lütfen	please
teşekkür ederim	thank-you
sağ ol!	health be! (informal way of expressing thanks)
iyi günler	good day
iyi geceler	good night
iyi akşamlar	good evening
günaydın	good morning
afiyet olsun!	good appetite (said both before and after a meal)
özür dilerim	sorry
nasılsınız?	How are you?
iyiyim; siz nasılsınız?	I'm well, how are you?

VOCABULARY

evet	yes
hayır	no
yok	none, no

çok	many, very
çok pahalı	very expensive
çok ucuz	very cheap
güzel	beautiful
fena	bad
iyi	good
kahve	coffee, coffee-house
çay	tea
bira	beer
şarap	wine
şeker	sugar
su	water
ekmek	bread
yumurta	egg
peynir	cheese
tuz	salt
hesap	bill
büyük	big
küçük	small
yavaş yavaş	slowly
çabuk	quick
yeter	enough
defol!	clear off!
buraya gel!	come here!
burda	just here
orda	over there
kapalı	closed
açık	open

PHRASES

istiyorum	I want
istemiyorum	I don't want
çay istiyorum	I want tea

çay istemiyorum	I don't want tea
etsiz yemek istiyorum	I want food without meat
(More politely)	
çay, lütfen	tea, please
içtim	I have drunk
yedim	I have eaten
iyi yedim	I have eaten well
gördüm	I have seen
ödedim	I have paid
var mı?	Is there?
ekmek var mı?	Is there bread?
ne kadar?	How much?
nerelisiniz?	Where are you from?
İngilizim	I am English
Amerikalıyım	I am American
İstanbul'a gitmek istiyorum	I want to go to Istanbul
Ankara'ya gitmek istiyorum	I want to go to Ankara

NUMBERS

1	bir
2	iki
3	üç
4	dört
5	beş
6	altı
7	yedi
8	sekiz
9	dokuz
10	on
11	onbir
12	oniki

20	yirmi
30	otuz
40	kırk
50	elli
60	altmış
70	yetmiş
80	seksen
90	doksan
100	yüz
1,000	bin
1,000,000	milyon

WRITING A LETTER

When writing a letter, you may write in English on the grounds that the person to whom you address it can find a translator. The address, however, must be written correctly. The name comes first, followed by the street, the number of the building in the street, and then the number of the apartment within the building. After this comes the name of the apartment, the district and the town. *Sayın* is usually abbreviated to *Sn.*, *Sokak*, meaning 'street' to *Sok*, Apartment to *Apt.* Zip codes have been recently introduced but they are not strictly necessary. If used, they are usually added before the town.

Sn Mehmet Akıllı...... name
Dar Sok 24/10......... name of street and number
Ufak apt. .... name of apartment
Kavaklıdere............. district
TR-06700 Ankara .... zipcode and town

To address a letter to a village, it is enough to have

the person's name, village (köy), sub-province (ilçe), and province (il). Thus

Sn. Mehmet Akıllı ..... name
Yeşil köyü .... village
Akpınar .... sub-province
Malatya .... province

Other relevant Turkish words are **adı** – name; **soyadı** – surname; **adres** – address; **mahalle** or **semt** – district: **kent** – town; **şehir** – city; **ülke** – country. Useful words when filling out forms are **memleket** – country of origin; **doğum tarihi** – date of birth; **meslek** – profession.

Turkish Words Used In The Text

ahdak	vow (religious)
arkadaş	friend or acquaintance
ayıp	shameful
ayran	a drink consisting of yoghurt mixed with water and salt
balo	large gathering to celebrate a marriage
bay	'Mr' (neologism) used before a man's surname
bayan	'Mrs' (neologism) used before a woman's surname
bey	'Mr' used after a man's given name (not their surname)
börek	stuffed pastry
büfe	snack-bar
cami	mosque
cin	gin
çay	tea
davul	drum
dolmuş	collective taxi
fez	Ottoman felt hat, now worn only by boys at their circumcision celebrations.
hanım	Lady, used after a woman's given name (not their surname)
hindi	Turkey (bird)

iftar	meal celebrating the break of fast during Ramazan
il	province
ilçe	sub-province
imam	mosque prayer leader
ithal	imported
jirit	jousting game played on horseback
kahve	coffee (also used to describe a place where tea or coffee is drunk)
konyak	cognac
Kurban bayramı	feast of sacrifice
merhaba	hello!
meze	starter (of a meal)
mihrab	niche oriented toward Mecca in a mosque
muzlu süt	banana milk
nar	pomegranate
pide	nan bread
pilav	cooked rice, served with main dishes
portakal suyu	orange juice
rakı	strong alcoholic drink
Ramazan	Ramadan (Month during which many people fast)
sade	plain (coffee)
sayın	'Dear' (title – as in when beginning a letter)
saygı	respect
simit	circles of bread topped with sesame seeds
sünnet	circumcision

sütlü muz	see *muzlu süt*
Şeker bayramı	Feast of Sweets (held to mark the end of Ramadan)
şekerli	sugared (coffee)
şenlik	festival
tarikat	Islamic brotherhood
tekke	Monastic centre of a brotherhood
tost	toasted sandwich
vakıf	charitable foundation
yazlık	summer house
yemek	food (vb. to eat)
yerli	local
zurna	folk reed instrument similar to an oboe

Further Reading

There is no one general book on modern Turkish society. However, Baron Kinross, *Atatürk: the rebirth of a nation*, London: Weidenfeld and Nicholson, 1964, gives a good description of Atatürk's life. Bernard Lewis' quite masterly *The Emergence of Modern Turkey*, London: Royal Institute of International Affairs, 1961 is still the best general account of the formation of the Republic. Erik Zürcher's *Turkey, A Modern History*, London: Tauris, 1994 gives a chronological account nearly up to the present day, Martin van Bruinessan's *Agha, Shaikh, and State*, London: Z books describes the history and society of Eastern Turkey, whilst Paul Stirling's *Turkish Village*, London: Weidenfeld and Nicholson, 1964, gives the clearest picture of life in a traditional community. Of the many books on Istanbul, Zeynep Çelik's *The Remaking of Istanbul : Portrait of an Ottoman City in the Nineteenth Century*, California, University of California Press, 1993 is very informative.

Facts About Turkey

Lying partly in Europe, but mostly in Asia, Turkey's geographical position gives it a significant influence in the Mediterranean, Black Sea and Middle East. For example, it guards the sea passage between the Black Sea and the Mediterranean which runs through the Bosphorus, Sea of Marmara and the Dardanelles

For a thousand years Turkey was the hub of the Byzantine Empire, and for 500 years it was the centre of the Ottoman Empire. Today, it provides NATO with key support in what is known as Europe's south-eastern flank.

Geography

Asian Turkey (Anatolia) is dominated by two mountain ranges - the Pontus mountains in the north and the Taurus mountains in the south which converge in the east rising to a height of 5165m. at mount Ararat (supposedly the resting place of Noah's Ark). The mountain ranges are separated by a high, semi-desert plateau, with the coastal regions being very fertile. The coast has a Mediterranean climate whereas the interior has very cold, snowy winters and hot, dry summers. Thrace, the other much smaller region, located on the European mainland, is fertile agricultural land with a Mediterranean climate. Total land area is 779.5 sq.km.

With a population of over 63 million, Turkey is the most populous country in the Middle East. The Turkish people are racially diverse, many being refugees or descendants of refugees, often from the Balkans, or other territories once under Russian rule. Almost the entire population is Muslim (99 per cent) with the ethnic mix being Turkish 80 per cent, Kurdish 17 per cent, 3 per cent other. Turkish is the official language; other languages spoken are Kurdish, Arabic, Circassian and Armenian.

The capital of modern Turkey is Ankara (not Istanbul), with sovereignty being vested in the Grand National Assembly, the sole legislative assembly; the days of rule under the Sultans being long passed. Since 1984, the southeastern region of Turkey has been the scene of a civil war waged by elements of the Kurdish minority demanding independence.

Turkey's economy has been thriving since the early 1980s, especially in textiles, manufacturing (including iron, steel and metals), construction and, increasingly, tourism. Germany is the biggest importer of Turkish exports taking nearly 25 per cent, followed by the US and Italy. Just under half the population continue to work in agriculture, followed by the services sector (31%) and Industry (21%).

Ancient Wonders

Turkey had two of the so-called seven wonders of the ancient world: the tomb of King Mausolus at Halicarnassus (now Bodrum), and the Temple of Artemis at Ephesus. Other historic sites are at Tarsus, the birthplace of St Paul, while much of the Aegean coast exhibits considerable quantities of Greek remains, including the site of Troy near Canakkale.

The 'father of modern Turkey' Mustafa Kemel, who later took the surname Atatürk, became the president of the republic in 1923 and ruled Turkey, virtually as a dictatorship, until his death in 1938. In order to project the then backward Muslim state into a modern, Western-style country of the twentieth century, he separated religion and state, abolished polygamy, banned men from wearing the fez, and discouraged women from wearing the veil.

Everyone under the age of 40 was required to go to classes to learn a new Latin alphabet for the Turkish language. In addition, Atatürk decreed that everyone must have a surname.

Index